A1

MW01166942

From God

Absolutely Non- Refundable, Paid in full with the Blood of Jesus the Christ

All scripture quotations are from the *KING JAMES VERSION; our directional pathway to live in God's full abundance. The HOLY BIBLE.*

All rights are reserved. Absolutely any, part of this book may not be reproduced in absolutely any form of documentation, copying, printing, reviewing, or re-production, unless with written notice of permission from the publisher.

Printed in the United States of America

Copyright by: Parice C. Parker 2007 with The Copyright of Congress

ISBN # 0-9787162-5-6

Fountain of Life Publisher's House

Cover Design & Illustrations by: Parice Parker

Author: Parice Parker

Editor: F. O. L. P. H.

A Precious Gift From God

A Precious Gift From God

*Absolutely Non- Refundable,
Paid in full with the Blood of
Jesus the Christ*

Table of Contents

Introduction

Chapters

Parice C. Parker

A Precious Gift From God

Introduction:

Just when you think, you have been forgotten and needing fulfillment, God will present you with a very special gift. A gift is normally given to you by surprise, in most cases they are presented to uplift, encourage and to inspire. A gift from God should always be appreciated, because it is priceless. God worked miraculously, just to give you and I the most precious divine gift of all. You will never know what all God has packed in this Gift until you unwrap it and receive it with gladness in your heart. This gift is absolutely non-refundable and packed with shipping power from The Most High. It is The Anointed at large and it's powered directly from Heaven to you. This gift is the most valuable gift you will ever receive. It is perfect, it will satisfy all your needs. So therefore take upon this opportunity, unwrap your gift and live your life more abundantly.

"If today was your last day on your job,

how prepared would you be" ?

Chapter One

Recognizing Your Gift

There are so many reasons that God gives us gifts. Your gift may come through a celebration or special occasion. He always knows how to keep our hearts stayed in Him. You also may recognize it when you are going through a terrible storm or something traumatic happens in your life. He always bring forth our gifts during our most needed times. I remember when I first recognized one of my gifts. I was so angry with the way my life was, I just began to write. The many temptations that tried to tempt me, I resisted them as I heavily endured. So as my anguish was still building, I could only release it to a pen and a piece of paper. Once I was finished I read it aloud and I could not stop writing. It became my first book. "Aggravated Assault On Your Mind". I realized, Gods purpose is to make me feel special, during my most trying times. It is something how He gives us gifts. However, each time God gave me a gift it was the time I most needed to be strengthen. God has a mighty way of surprising us. 11 Samuel 22:40 says, For thou has girded me with strength to battle: them that rose up against me hast thou subdued under my feet. Your gift will be your power to overcome once you recognize how valuable it is. There is so much power in your gift that it will cause you to win all your battles, even before your battle really appears. Just as David, he was one that was extremely gifted in many ways, from being one of the greatest inspirational writers of all times until he was able to inspire His Lord of Lords and Kings of Kings. His gifts caused heaven to keep him covered. God is mighty and He owns the fortress of true happiness. He owns every good deed, every true conquer and knows every life destiny. It was one occasion when I wanted to turn back. I begin to grow tired in trying to accomplish. It seemed the more I was praying and trying the worst my life appeared. The more I went to church the higher my mountains grew and the more I testified the more my life seemed to fall. I begin to ask myself, "Why, why, why should I continue living right and everything else is going so wrong?" It just seemed that I was more blessed when I lived in the world. However, a voice said to me, "Utilize Your Gifts." The truth was right there in my hearing and I know that it was the Spirit of God speaking to me. At that moment, I was so angry I begin to write out my feelings. I opened my heart to a piece of paper and allowed the pen to have its way. Then I read it aloud, it was remarkable and instantly I felt so much better. As I read what I had written out of my heart. I realized that it was not I, but it was God writing through me. Every since then, I begin to write. I realized God gave me the gift of writing to

keep my mind focused on Him. He wants us to speak
to Him with our gifts. He wants to be inspired, that
is why David was the apple of his eye, because
David took the time to inspire God. Many of us are
so busy going to God for a need until we don't take
the time to encourage heaven to begin a work on
our behalf. It is absolutely, non-refundable – it's
His heart. God has wrapped His heart in it and this
Gift will bring you joy during your times of sorrow.
Your gift is to inspire Him, no matter what you are
going through. He will gain greater recognition
through the utilization of appreciating your gift. We
all have many types of gifts and your gift is unique,
He wants to be inspired. I know sometimes it's hard
for us to use our gifts during troubled times, but
truly it's the best time for your gift to expand. It can
be a marriage separation, a hard fall in life, a death
or even some other unexpected life destruction – it
does not matter. He wants our true trust in Him. If
you believe that no matter how big your situation is,
but that your God is greater than any situation and
circumstance then you will begin to inspire Him so

that He will change your situation. He gives us gifts for a purpose and He wants to be inspired.

Understand there is drawing power in the utilization of your gift. First of all it let's God know how much you appreciate Him. Secondly it will cause someone else's burdens to be lifted. In addition, thirdly it will cause someone else to recognize Him through you. Every time you use your gift someone will be encouraged. I believe within all of my heart that David truly pleased God, despite of His sins – He pleased God. Often times many put their focus on their sin, until they can't cause God to be moved. However, we all have fallen short at one time or another and we should always continue to try trusting God more. There is only one way to overcome sin and that is to keep on trying to please God. David had a heart desire to satisfy God through His writings. Every song he song testified of His God. Out of all David did, his greatest accomplishment is the Glory that he is still causing God to receive, even until this day. That is the same thing that God wants from you today, is to inspire Him. David simply knew how to inspire God, and he didn't stop until he did. Romans 12:6 says, Having then gifts differing according to the grace that is given to us, whether prophecy, let us prophesy according to the proportion of faith; David's faith was mighty in God, because he knew how to anticipate God to move in his life. He was a believer in God's word and his faith was proportioned well in Him. I mean absolutely nothing caused David to stop trying to please God, no sin not even a battle, circumstance or a situation. His purpose was set in His mind to overcome and He always gave God that Glory to be his burden carrier. He continuously inspired God.

Understand your gift was given to you with a supernatural intention to develop something wonderful out of you. Once you recognize your gift, you need to seek the purpose of it. And you should not stop until God says, He is satisfied. For different reasons God gives us different gifts, and behind your special gift God develops it within you uniquely. No one could ever receive, respect and honor your gift as you can. Your gift was specially designed just for your life. In addition, no one could appreciate it or utilize it as God would have you too. It has a purpose to fulfill your life with many wonderful things, as it will give God greater recognition. Truly, it's main purpose is to inspire God. Often times we are not prepared to accept our gifts in the manner God will give them to us. In addition, sometimes we do not understand how effective our gifts will be in our lives, less known someone else's. There were times I wanted to give up. Yes, I wanted to throw in the towel, but my gifts saved me. When I realized the gift of writing was upon me, every time I grew to anger or depressed I begin to write. The Holy Spirit wanted to develop me and God enriched me. The writings were my inspiration. Not only did they inspire me, but I believe they too inspired God. As I wrote tension was released, my anger grew to calmness and peace would surrender me. My life at the time was appointed to writing and as I wrote God delivered me. Your gift has a purpose to cause you to overcome. It does not matter what your gift's are just utilize them, they will serve many great purposes in your life well as others. I Timothy 4:14 says, Neglect not the gift that is in thee, which was given thee by prophecy, with the laying on of the hands of the presbytery.

Often times we are so caught up into our nothing of a lives, until we simply neglect our gifts. Notice, every time you neglect your gifts, you also cause negligence to become the leader of your prosperity. Just think, once negligence is your life leader then so is failure, bondage, corruption, dead works, no vision and no great rewards. Look upon your gift, it is valuable – actually it is truly priceless. God wants you to utilize the gift(s) that He has given you, because He wants to bring you out of bondage. He wants you sitting high and He wants everyone to look upon you and say, "Now he or she is more than a conquer". When you step *through any entrance, He wants many to notice that you are blessed and highly favored. Give others a reason to desire after righteousness, let them see God through you. Be the one that will cause a chain reaction, for people to seek God as though they have lost their minds.*

Imagine if you had the position in life as God has, think of all the prayers, heart desires, needs, burdens and so much more being put on Him daily. See, God instructs all that are heavy laden to come to Him. None of us could actually be Him, but just imagine all that you put on Him in your life time, less known the whole world. All I know is that when I'm inspired it will motivate me, encourage my heart and make me feel extremely special. And once I feel extremely special I smile, I glow, I run and I become more than a conquer. Your gift is to make you and to satisfy Him every time you utilize it. Allow Him to know that you appreciate your gift and no matter what utilize it. I remember during this particular conference I began to sang and the people were amazed. It wasn't how I was singing, but it was the way I sung. I remember when I first began singing people truly picked on me, but I kept on singing. No one knew, what I was going through or either what The Lord was currently doing in my life. However when hell raise up in your life, your gift will also raise you up. I have never sung in that particular manner, until this conference. At the time my life was going through the fire and my voice was the way I testified. See, I just had a stroke at only 36, being paralyzed on my right side, but I did not let it stop me from praising my Lord. Praise The Lord I was healed. I utilized my gift with a different heart desire and a deeper strength, from the bottom of my belly was my voice heard. One came up to me and said, "sing Pastor Parker sing". She said, "yokes are destroyed and burdens are lifted when you sing". I have never received such a powerful comment about my singing as that. Your gift have power to loose someone that is confined, to free someone from bondage and to cause someones hell to be denounced. You must recognize the power that is in your gift, it doesn't matter who you are or even what you have done, utilize your gift. Now what if I would have allowed the crucial comments of others throughout the years, hinder my progress? Though many laughed at me, they didn't understand all that I had went through. I sing to be released, it's a way I praise and a way I'm freed. It is also a way I communicate with Jehovah. I realized no matter what, people are going to criticize you whether you are doing good or bad. I think many of days if I would have kept my mouth shut because someone told me to, would God have been satisfied with me? I didn't come to satisfy man, but I am born to satisfy my Glorious Creator. 1John 4:4 says, Ye are of God, little children, and have overcome them: **because greater is he that is in you, than he that is in the world.**

There wasn't one battle that David could fight alone, he needed heavenly strength for every battle. He did not let anything or anyone stop him. His main purpose was to gain the heart of God. Understand in gaining one's heart, you must try to reach for it. You will do all that is necessary to obtain the love you desire, by doing what you need to in order to receive it. Nothing will stop you, not even sin will get in your way. That is why we are able to bend, God knew we would need to bow in forgiveness – over and over again. Once He forgives you, it is done – so therefore move on. David knew that he would always overcome, because He knew who He served. 11 Samuel 7:26 says, And let thy name be magnified for ever, saying, The Lord of hosts is the God over Israel: and let the house of thy servant David be established before thee.

God has promised me so many wonderful things, what about you? Hold on to His promises and His word, for they will never fail you. Remember the more you use your gifts, the more He will be acknowledged to be God over your life. And the more He is exalted through your gifts, the more he will be motivated to move in your life. So *therefore recognize the power that is in your gift, unwrap it and show it to the world. Be proud of it and let it be seen, heard and known until you inspire God. 1John 4:4 says, Ye are of God, little children, and have overcome them: **because greater is he that is in you, than he that is in the world.***

Chapter Two

The Value Of Your Gift

When God speaks to you, know His voice. It is amazing, how the enemy will come in just to destroy you. He finds his way to sneak into your life, just so your gift will be unnoticed. He does not want you to utilize what God has given you, because he would lose great recognition. Come on, if you switch sides you will be too blessed to be over stressed and then your life won't be in a mess. John 10:10 says, The thief cometh not, but to steal, and to kill, and to destroy: I am come that they

might have life, and that they might have life more
abundantly. Many people currently have a life, but
are they living more abundantly? Just look around
at the many people you know, many are having all
kinds of problems including yourself – what would
literally make you to want to live like them? Though
you have a life, is it what you desire? Do you have
everything in your life that your heart truly desire?
Just think for a moment. If the enemy can have his
way in your life, then you will not desire to utilize
your gift, think about it. That is why you must keep
your gift in the perfect place, always being
prepared to be used. Right now ask yourself these
questions, is my gift usable? Am I really ready to be
used by God and who or what would I draw in for
Him? Can I inspire God? I know when I receive a
beautiful gift, I handle it with very special care.
Actually my first priority is to insure proper care
for the gift. Surely, God wants you to take care of
your gift(s), show Him how much you value it or
them. Would you leave a 5 carat princess cut
diamond sitting out for someone to steal or would

you store it away from the thieves? Understand one thing, the enemy have more than just him working trying to steal from you, he have many. You must keep your gifts protected, they are extremely valuable. They're so valuable, the enemy wants your gift's. Your gift posses life form that money can't buy and it has the potential to destroy hell out of someones life – including your own. Now look at that, not just yours but your seeds, the next generation and vice versa. Your gift is Divine and it's priceless. Your gift is so potent, until it will cause someone's heart to be turned on to Jesus. It is so valuable that it will evict hell out of someone's home, meaning sparing Jesus more hearts and saving more souls. Your gift also have the authority to make you rich, including all your seeds. Get to know the depth of the power that your gift posses. It is life threating. Proverbs 10:22 says, The blessings of the Lord, it maketh one rich, and he addeth no sorrow with it.

God wants you to know Him in depth through your heart intentions. Though often our hearts stray from the right intentions we must find our way back. David was one that found himself straying in many ways through many things, but his gifts was specially designed to inspire. As He song many noticed that he was outstanding, he mightily inspired the hearts of many. David loved his music and his heart was full of inspirations. Though his battles were great, his victories was even greater. David had many reasons to inspire God. Sometimes in life things will happen to get us off course, but just remember to get back on. Though the enemy tried to stopDavid, his mind was set on how powerful his God was. He knew he was being attacked from every angle, but utilizing his gifts kept him protected. 11 Samuel 22:6 says, The sorrows of hell compassed me about; the snares of death prevented me; Understand, David knew that his enemies was great, but he also remembered how the Lord has previously brought him out. During our hell storms we too must remember our previous victories, our previous battles and know that it was only the Lord that has brought us through. A lot of people may not understand what you are going through and no one can tell it like you can. Regardless of what's going on in your life, do not allow the enemy to gain your victory. David was a true receiver of the word. Remember whatever goes in must come out. David received power every time he received a word from the Lord. As David received a word from the Lord he also received a moment of inspiration that caused him to gladly satisfy His Lord with utilizing his gifts. Only a receiver of great power can be a true warrior and an accomplisher of greater works. 1John 4:4 says, Ye are of God, little children, and have overcome them: **because greater is he that is in you, than he that is in the world.** You are what you are, and whatever enters, is what is going to come out. Psalms 34:1 says, I Will bless the Lord at all times, his praise shall continually be in my mouth. David knew there was only one place that he could get feed spiritually, and that was in the presence of The

Lord. So many people forsake the assembly of the saints when they are living in sin, until it will cause them to lose out on there abundance. I do not know about you, but I want my abundance of life. It is time out for scuffling, half way making it or barely surviving. Jesus came so that we might take part of the abundance. Though the enemy came for another purpose, I am going to live in the abundance – what about you? You have a choice and an opportunity, which one are you going to choose? Are you going to continue to desire to live more abundantly, or are you going to move forward; until you live in the abundance. He wants us to have the best that life has to offer. No, the enemy don't want you to want the best, because he wants you to be content in life. John 10:10 says, The thief cometh not, but for to steal, and to kill, and to destroy: I am come that they might have life, and that they might have it more abundantly. Why just live when you can live more abundantly. **Once you begin to live in the abundance, your faith is increased to a level that hell can't stop your praise.** *That is why, hell has* been trying to stop you in your tracks. Hell wants to disconnect you from living more abundantly and to disconnect you from your life promises. The enemy does not want you to utilize your gifts, because God will receive greater glory. Your gift is so valuable, many lives are depending on it. People in general look at there gifts as just a gift, but no your gift will incorporate abundance. IT WILL GIVE ANOTHER AN OPPORTUNITY TO LIVE MORE ABUNDANTLY. That is why the enemy has tried to stop you from using your gift. See, as I use my gifts my heart is relaxed in Him. My mind is focused in Him and Peace is mine. Your gift holds the power of life and death, it is valuable. Think about who inspired Billy Graham through a word of encouragement to preach the gospel or who caused him to acknowledge life through the word. What about Martin Luther King, who inspired him through a word of encouragement to become a freedom fighter. There is freedom power in your gift. Do not let the enemy keep your gift suppressed any longer, allow God to receive the glory. Psalms

29:4 says, The voice of the Lord is powerful; the voice of the Lord is full of majesty. David was one that constantly heard from the Lord, it is His voice that will keep you motivated. Allow nothing to keep you away from hearing Him, it is not worth it. I know at one time in my life I needed a word from the Lord like a baby needed milk to survive. I was hungry. My life was being tormented by hell left and right, but I stayed in the word. I felt as though I was being beaten alive, every where I turned I received a blow from the enemy, the word gave me new life. No matter what I never want to grow so big that I can't be a receiver. A receiver is one that is feed and I want to be as "Spiritually Feed & Spiritually Developed as I can be". The more I'm feed power is the more I can handle the blows of life. That is why it is so valuable to continually to be feed the Word, so that your gift can grow. Nothing can destroy the word, it will live forever and ever. David was constantly being encouraged by the Word of God because He was a Praiser. Psalms 29:4 says, The voice of the Lord is powerful; the voice of the Lord is full of majesty. A praiser will constantly hear from the Lord. Once a praiser hear from The Lord they get excited because they are able to see God working in their life. Every time God speaks to me, he excites my praise, because He simply motivates my heart. When He speaks my mind is off my troubles and on my blessing. I don't know about you, but I have come too far for me to turn around now. I have also praised too much for me to think that God doesn't have the power to turn my troubles into a magnificent praise report. I refuse to give the enemy my praise, nothing interferes with my praise because my abundance is in my praise. 1 Corinthians 2:9 says, But as it is written, Eye hath not seen, nor ear heard, neither have entered into the heart of man, the things which God hath prepared for them that love him. Though I haven't received them yet, I know that it is so. All I need is His word and His word is enough to motivate my praise. Just as David, though he entered his battles his victory was in his praise.

A Precious Gift From God

It doesn't matter who we are or who we are not, we all want to be loved. David utilize his gifts, no matter what. David didn't even allow sin to stop him from trying to please God. So many think we can get ourselves together, it is impossible. However, all things are possible through Him. We are all human, we have tendencies to quit, give up, and sometimes we just get tired of trying. Most definetly, we still must not quit. It was my gift of writing that tried my faith. My gift tried my patience as it caused me to get more spiritually fit to overcome. It caused my heart to hearken towards God more. It sat me down and caused my heart well as my ears to be attentative towards God. However, through it all, I was inspired to run. My heart was consoled each time I utilized my gifts, they have turned my life completely around.

The enemy does not want you to use your gift, that is why He has attacked your faith. He wants you to think it to be impossible. 1John 4:4 says, Ye are of God, little children, and have overcome them: **because greater is he that is in you, than he that is in the world.** I looked at myself plenty of times and I was my worst critic. Often times I said, "I cannot write." I gave myself more excuses not to utilize my gifts, then I did to utilize them. I bashed myself and constantly criticized my writings. I want you to know every time we bash our gifts we bash Jesus. I constantly said, "I am a nobody, who's going to want my books and I cannot write." Boy, I put myself down more than I exalted God. I did not want to trust that God had given me the gift of writing for the world to see. For years, I kept the gift of writing to myself. Surely, I shared it with a few family members and friends, but I was not prepared to share it with the world. So every now and again, I began to write. However, one day I realized if I write only 15 minutes a day then soon I could finish this book. At that time, I was writing the book "Aggravated Assault On Your Mind." Then I continued to go through more life struggles. One day God gave me a few figures to add up, and it astonished me. Surely if I had what He told me to *calculate I would not be suffering financially today. Immediately I begin to write more, I grew consistent with writing books. I stopped giving myself excuses because those excuses caused me to not utilized my gift of writing. Every time you down yourself, you show God that you do not appreciate your gift. Today God wants you to receive your gift and then He wants you to adore it. Romans 12:6 says, Having then gifts differing according to the grace that is given to us, whether prophecy, let us prophesy according to the proportion of faith; Remember faith comes by hearing and not by sight. Once you hear what the Lord is speaking, then your eyes are able to see it even before you receive it. Instantly in your belly you will feel the flow of blessings, once you receive what the Lord is speaking to you. David was one that received all that God had for him, it didn't matter how large it was – he believed Him for it. His faith was to the extreme in the Lord, that is why his praise was so potent to inspire God. I do not know what your gift's are, but I know they will bless heaven. Think of the many great spiritual leaders that would have never appreciated their gifts, how many might not have been delivered today. In addition, the many gifted inspirational singers along with songwriters, perhaps many people would not have received a peace of mind. What ever your gift's are God wants you to utilize them for His glory. He does not want you to be ashamed of it, but He wants it to be used. Once you begin to unwrap your gift, you will realize the true value of it. It will reach many hearts and cause many to become more than a conquer. God has given you something unique and He wants you to trust His judgments. He chose you and only you, He gave this gift. Ephesians 4; 7 says, But unto every one of us is given (opportunity to obtain something special from God) grace according to the measure (the unlimited measures) of the gift (perfection of Jesus) of Christ.*

David is already known to be more than a conquer, but no matter what he had to come up against David held on to Gods unchanging hands. One that reads is wise, one that seeks shall find and one that ask shall receive. David did it all. He realized that in order for him to just make it through the next day, that he needed to be strengthened. Without power a man is nothing and David longed for power to overcome. David also knew that His Father was rich, meaning God was his every resource. 1John 4:4 says, Ye are of God, little children, and have overcome them: ***because greater is he that is in you, than he that is in the world.*** *Only God can lead you, guide you and establish you. So therefore, David took upon every opportunity that His Father gave him to learn of his gift(s) and to utilize them. Make sure you keep your gift(s) usable for Him, because they will inspire heaven.*

Chapter Three

Your Gift Will Release Pressure

One reason, a gift is so special is

because of the happiness it will bring forth. Notice
that when you are happy, your day goes better and
your mind feels free. The enemy knows that
happiness brings laughter and that is good. He also
knows that it gives our hearts joy. So therefore, he
doesn't want you to get too comfortable in

happiness because you would desire it more often. Happiness is powerful, because then one is completely free. Allow your gift to bring you happiness, well as God. David made God happy every time he song praises and every time he battled, God was exalted. Your gift can make Him happy too. When you look upon your gift, you will be able to see the blessings that will come from them. Your gift will cause you to live more abundantly through Jesus Christ. Luke 6:21 says, Blessed are ye that hunger now: for ye shall be filled. Blessed are ye that weep now: for ye shall laugh. Though your troubles may be great, know that God is greater. Though your tears are flowing, know that your laughter is on it's way. I remember when I was truly going through this awful or deal, boy I was so frustrated and I didn't think I was going to make it, but regardless of how bad things looked I kept my faith. Sometimes during crucial times of our life, sure we want to give in and most definetly we get tired of trying, but just know that your day is coming soon. David was a warrior and a great one at that, because he didn't fear. Often we allow fear to embark on our happiness. All because we are afraid to move forward. One thing I can say about David, is that truly he never needed an army because his faith was perfectly proportioned in God. Ephesians 4; 8 says, Wherefore he saith, "WHEN HE ASCENDED UP ON HIGH, HE LEAD CAPTIVITY CAPTIVE, AND GAVE GIFTS UNTO MEN".

Another one of Davids famous gifts was winning, he wouldn't settle for less. It did not matter what he had to go against, David wanted his day of joy. He wouldn't let absolutely anything stop him from winning. There is complete joy in winning, but we will get back to that in the last chapter. Understand when you win, victory is yours. When Jesus died on the cross for our sins and rose up with all power. As long as you call on Him, nothing can hold you back. Jesus holds the key to release you today from all captivity. God has given you gifts to set you free from bondage. You have to understand that every strong hold over you, every pressure that is within you - He can release from you. Your freedom, your happiness, your life comes through the determination that you have to believe in the power of Jesus. Everyday Jesus allows someone through his or her gift to be set free. Once the Spirit of Truth is accepted within your heart, then shall you receive your freedom? Jesus didn't allow the circumstances that rose up against Him, to hold Him down. And He didn't allow the people that went against Him to stop Him and neither did David. No matter your battle, know your God He is all powerful. David knew him as a Shepherd. Psalms 23:1 says, The Lord is my shepherd I shall not want. And believe me, God took great care of him.

Sometimes we let people control our gift that God has given us. We seek the approval of man and not the attention of God as we need to. For years I was trying to stand up to the standards of man as being a preacher, just wanting them to see that God really did call me to minister. I wanted so badly for so many preachers to acknowledge me as a minister of the Gospel. Many of times during our in house fellowships, at our church I felt so uncomfortable. I always thought that being a minister more people would show you greater love. However, the longer I stayed in ministry the more I realized it is not about them or me. I often said to myself, "if God was for me then who shall be against me". For many of years I struggled in the ministry. I struggled with the gift that God had given me, trying to prove to man. One day I finally woke up and said, who cares as long as my God cares that is all I need. I wanted Him to care, Him to notice and I decided to please Him. God did not give me that particular calling to prove myself to man, but to bring forth glad tidings to the broken and wounded hearts. There are so many people dying daily due towards lack of inspirations and here I was worrying about trying to prove to man that God called me. I turned that thing around and decided to inspire God so that men can inspire

*Him too. When someone is down uplift them, we live
in a world of many broken spirits. So many people
need to truly be inspired. I realized that man did not
call me, but my Father which is in Heaven called
me to preach the gospel. I had to grow up, mature
and developed. You too must realize that God gave
you a special gift and there is a purpose for every
God given gift. Satisfy Him and watch Him satisfy
you, David knew that too. To you that mission will
seem to be impossible until you find the purpose for
your gift. Make God happy by using your gift to
bring Him glory. As I continued through the years
of ministry, I was developed more in books as I
wrote. You will never imagined how far your gift
can take you, until you be obedient and utilize it for
Him. Allow your gift to bless your life well as
others, it will bring forth greater things. Proverbs
10:22 says, The blessings of the Lord, it maketh
rich, and he addeth no sorrow with it.*

*Often times God will already have
given you a gift and you do not even notice it*

because you have a zillion and one things on your mind. Understand God cannot present Himself fully unto you, until your mind is free and clear. Your mind must be in a position to receive your gift, when He presents you with it. He wants you to recognize that He is giving you something greater. John 14:17 says, Even the Spirit of truth; whom the world cannot receive, because it seeth him not, neither knoweth him: but ye know him; for he dwelleth with you, and shall be in you.

You are not an orphan because you are a child of God. Surely, the enemy is trying to tempt you through every stronghold he has over you right now. However, God has not left you alone He is only giving you a backbone to stand on your gift. He is giving you one of the greatest gifts of all, the opportunity to explore – (True Life) His Son Jesus the Christ. The truth is that everyone does not believe and will not receive Jesus, because they do not understand Him. No matter how high you search, how low you fall until you receive Jesus in your life, no Gift that God will give you - will be fully developed? Through His Blood, you are now receiving strength, might, capability and your spiritual realm is only growing wider, deeper and stronger. When you are developing spiritually, sometimes no matter how much church you are getting, how active you are in the ministry or even your title, we all get to a point where we just need God that much. God knows our weakness and He knows just how much you and I truly can bear.

David was a true warrior, he stood up towards his enemies and won every battle. 11 Samuel Chapter Nine discuss how many victories David had in just one Chapter. Now wonder if David would have feared going against his enemies, he would have still been pressured? When you really want your pressures of life released, you will fight to win. You will stand in faith and utilize what God has given you to the fullest. Now what if David would have thought he wasn't strong enough to fight against the

Philistines, or what If he would have aborted himself in battle? Now if you read this chapter, after each battle David was richly blessed after each victory. He would have also aborted his blessing. David kept in mind how great God is, he knew Him as a shield. So therefore, David was always protected by the Greatest Life Protector. Psalms 3:3 says, But thou, O Lord, art a shield for me; my glory, and the lifter up of mine head. Even when you are going through, He will lift you up. That gift that you have is your pressure releaser. It doesn't matter what you are going through, just know that you are an overcomer. Now allow your gift to take you to your next level, gain your next victory until you triumph in life. Use your gift to satisfy Jesus and believe me, He will surely make you laugh.

Chapter Four

God Is Depending On Your Gift

God wants to pull you away

from the ordinary crowd that is why He did not give
you an ordinary gift. God is a God that does
extraordinary works by calling you out of an
ordinary crowd. Matthew 20:16 says, So the last
shall be first, and the first last; for many be called,
but few chosen. He called you because you possess
an extraordinary quality that is why He has given

*you this gift. It will bring Him Extraordinary Glory. Can you imagine being that **One** that will cause God to receive Extraordinary Glory? David did, and he was forever blessed. He wants to anoint you so that this work assignment that He has given you will be a Divine Work. Allow the Anointing To Surface as you exercise your gift(s). The assignment that God has given you through your gift is a secular work. It is for The GREAT I AM to be magnified in a work that He expects of you. This gift is yours, it was assigned just for you to utilize it. God expects great things from you, which is why He has called you out of an ordinary crowd. When God appointed you, He looked at your qualifications as He checked your background and allowed you to pass a numerous amount of test. Your test has qualified you for this work. You met all of His qualifications, now He requires something more powerful of you. God no longer wants you to be just an ordinary person. **He wants you to be that peculiar vessel - the one that can and will get the job done.** You have **"Can Do Power"** in your gift,* *every time you think you can't, just say it aloud, **"I** **Can Do This".** Deuteronomy 14:2 says, For thou art an holy people unto the LORD thy God, and the LORD hath chosen thee to be a peculiar people unto himself, above all the nations that are upon the earth. He has thought mighty highly of you to even choose you for this work, now He wants you to think higher of yourself. He wants this work assignment that He has given you to be complete. I have told many people through my years in ministry that if you don't believe in yourself, then no one else will. If you don't want to achieve for greater, then no one is going to reach higher for you. In addition, if you want something done right, then just do it yourself. But this one person told me, I can show you better than I can tell you – just watch my feet. He wants you to be more powerful and full with The Anointing Performance from the work of your hands. It is your production time to prove to yourself that God has assigned you this work. You will most definitely know that this vision was from God once you finish it. God is a God of life and* until it becomes to life form it is a dead work. He wants your gift to survive, He wants it to live. Moreover, faith without works is dead. God is a faithful God and every word that proceeds out of His mouth will bring forth a production of truth, it will be fully developed and it will be known that God did it, just because He spoke it. God is a God that has mastered Life to the fullness and only He has the Power to raise the dead. Exercise your gift. Matthew 8:22 says, But Jesus said unto him, Follow me; and let the dead bury the dead.

Let your gift live. Keeping your gift buried is like burying life alive. Someone needs to see your gift or feel it come to life, because someone is depending on your gift to survive. There is hope in your gift, joy for another's heart and love that will caress a soul. You would be amazed of what a good song will do in someone's life and how a good doctor will save a life. Your gift is needed and someone needs it more than you. Allow the Anointing to surface through utilizing your gift. For

years I actually allowed my gifts to stay buried,
because of lack of exercising my gifts. Perhaps the
gift that God has given you will help many in there
time of need. Now look upon that gift and ask your
self, is it worth living? And if so, begin to utilize it
and let God give it life. Just as God assigned Noah
to build the Ark, He did not ask Noah's son, nor his
wife or any other friend or family member. God had
this assignment set-aside especially for Noah, not
Moses, not Jeremiah nor Mary, but Noah. He knew
that only Noah could build such a sizable Ark that
met all of His special specifications. There was only
one that God could depend on to build the ark and
it could only be Noah. Perhaps if God would have
called on Moses, he probably would have gotten
tired too soon. Jeremiah may have been shouting
too much and he too could not have finished the
work. Mary would not have had the arm strength,
the building techniques to handle such a workload.
God knew that she could be a virgin and birth baby
Jesus. A work that God has chosen for you to do, is
just for you. Luke 7:14 says, And he came and

touched the bier: and they that bare him stood still.
And he said, Young man, I say unto thee, Arise.
Whatever it is that God is expecting you to do, it
cannot happen until you decide to finish your work.
God chose Moses to lead many out of bondage, but
He only allowed Noah to lead 8 including himself
through building the ark. God knew just how much
Moses could bare vice versa Noah. Remember as
you work this vision with your hands, God won't put
no more on you than you can bear. However, to
many the eight being led to safety look like nothing
compared to the amount of people that Moses lead
out of captivity. Well if it had not been for the 8 that
Noah led out, then this world would not even be in
existence today. Because it is the eight that Noah
built the ark for including all the animals that he
led out through following precise instructions from
God, is the reason you and I are here today. Now
what if Noah would have just led the 8 out, but
forgot the animals or built a boat instead an ark.
God intended him to build an ark because a boat
would not have been able to hold it all, or survive

the rainstorm. I believe that now and days we want to do many things our way after we have received our gifts from God. We sometimes want the easy way out, but with God there is no easy way out. God is a God of firm instructions and every instruction is for a Divine Purpose. Just as David stood to battle with the Philistines, it wasn't easy – but he fought until he won. When he went against Moab, it wasn't easy – but David fought until he gained victory. No battle is easy, but the victory is always rewarding. Fight until you win. However, what and whom Noah saved through His obedience to God was just enough to excite God to create again. It was just enough for God to make the world happen all over again. As we please God, He begins to please us more. He will make things that have died in our life come to life again. He will also make what has been washed away, come back greater in our life. I tell you we serve an awesome God. As we listen to Him He will give us the same precise instructions in order to release the fullness of our gifts. God has a plan for your gift to produce more life. Through your determined effort God is going to make some one else stand firmer, get motivated and most of all become usable forHim. Now notice that Noah did not focus on all the materials he needed, or the equipment to build such an ark, it was not available at His hands reach. But God brought the things as he needed them. Every piece of wood, every nail and everything else from starting at a low ground to giving him a ladder of hope as he built the ark higher. Today God wants your hope all the way up to the top of your vision. Take your mind off the needed things in order to make this work gain life. However, put your mind on the Powerful God that can touch any dead thing and bring it to a life form. Talk about all the needed materials Noah did not have, but he built the ark anyway compared to today's materials. David also knew Him as his Rock. Psalms 18:2 says, The Lord is my rock, and my fortress, any my deliverer; my God, my strength, in whom I will trust; my buckler, and my horn of my salvation, and my high tower.

Just as the widow woman walking with the crowd on her way to bury her only child, Jesus was in her by passing, but He did not by pass her. Jesus saw and felt her heart. Though her son was dead, lying in a coffin on the way to his burial ground, Jesus looked at the coffin and He spoke to her son and said, "Young man, I say unto thee, Arise. So the boy arose and as he arose he begin to talk, he talked his way out of death. That young man talked his way out of a dead mans coffin on the way to his burial ground. When the Lord speaks, it is so. No matter what you are going through, know that The Lord is speaking. Today Jesus say speak life. Speak it so, until that dead gift comes to life. Proverbs 15:4 says, A wholesome tongue is a tree of life: but a perverseness therein is a breach in the spirit. Allow the strong hold of the enemy that is binding down your vision hear what thus said the Lord. Speak to your gift and watch the death hold be removed in the name of Jesus. The power right now is in your tongue. Speak with power, use that power of Anointing and speak unto your vision. In the name of Jesus tell your gift to get up. Watch how movement begins to take place in your life. As that young man heard the voice of Jesus, he gained life because of The Anointing Power that was in the voice of the Lord. Sometimes if you cannot feel that anointing in your gift, then you must speak it in existence. If Jesus did, then so can you. However you choose to use the Anointing Powers of God, just use them. Right now claim your victory for your vision, speak to your gift in the name of Jesus, declare this work to be done. Matthew 12:34 says, O ye generations of vipers, how can ye being evil speak good things? For out of the abundance of the heart the mouth speaketh.

Your mind will be made up and you will be prepared to move forward. **Know that the power that is in JESUS name is considered to be The Accomplisher.** There is nothig that He have'nt accomplished and anything you need Him to accomplish, He will. He gives us the strenght to *excel in life, when we truly want to. It is time to make some needed changes within your life, to explore the true revelation of this gift that God has given you. Don't you want it to come to pass, if so then make some changes. These changes can only happen through the power that is in the name of JESUS. In addition, you must prepare yourself to do some things that you normally would'nt do. You can do it, just tell yourself every time you think you can't - that you can. There are expectations from God for you to finish, it is a work that has been specially formulated for every cell that God has formed within your body. This gift was specially created and made just for you. Every blood vessel, every bone structure and through every finger tip has God designed this, just for you. The structure of the cells is specifically designed for you to do it. There is no way around it, because once you begin, it will be complete. Just as God has given you this gift, He has also shown you your reward. Surely, you want to receive the full benefit of your reward. Think once God fulfills this gift. Philippians 2:2*

A Precious Gift From God

*says, Full fil ye my joy that ye be like minded, having the same love, being of one accord, of one mind; Of mighty works that will fill you with joy and that will allow a multitude to also rejoice in it after the finishing of it. Though this work is not complete yet, God said, **"Work It," "Finish It," and "Let It Surface"** because He has spoken it. Understand one thing, that this is the most valuable thing, when God gives an assignment it will go forth. Oh it's all going to happen, but you may not be the receiver of the reward unless you finish it. If you are obedient to the call of this work that God has given you, then you will be the receiver of this work reward. Look upon your hands one more time, notice its appearance and think of what could all come from it when you finish. God has certain duties that must be performed by certain servants. I have never known of a servant of the Lord that did not gain The Anointing or served Him powerless. These powers are designated only for the ones that **The Lord appoints** for the services that He need or want for a **True Divine Purpose**. The Lord will let it* be known after He has put His hands on you. There is absolutely no way to hide from the service call that God has given His appointed servers to do. God has given you a **Special Divine Assignment** that will lead, guide and be a light of truth for many to follow. He has a plan just for the gift He has given you. Your gift was planned to deliver. Believe me, God has a plan that will not fail even if you do. By now surely your vision has been made clear to you. Just note the facts, when God gives you a duty, then you will become His servant by answering the call of God. Many people look upon a calling as becoming a preacher, no that is not true. God has called many to duty, but they never cared to receive true instructions. Surely, God has called many to preach and teach but maybe not to lead. Today many run, and open up a church when that is not what God has called them to do. Sometimes we hear only part of the instructions, some can get so excited until they run before God finish giving the instructions. God gives us instructions to follow as He calls us to become His servants. We all have a *calling, God calls all of us to do some form of good service for Him, but many refuse to listen as He speaks. However, all calls are not called to preach nor teach the gospel. Some callings are for some form of charity. It could also be to start a new business that will offer more job opportunities. Moreover, some are just called to preach and teach the word of God expecting to bring forth glad tidings through the word. However, all callings will be a form of help, inspiration, encouragement and that will build up lives, through one-way or another. All visions are not just in the church, many are on the outside. Our duty is to build, inspire and to bring forth light in the world - through the many operable gifts of God. Be prepared to be used for the glory of God and continue to exercise your gifts.*

Chapter Five

Insure Your Gift (s)

*The Anointing is an appointment to gain Powers that can only flow from God for the calling of His servants. Believe me, God have servants in every good service of this life. Once God lay **His Hands Upon You,** then you are His. Often many try to run, but they simply can't hide from God. Your life will not be right until you obey Him. David was one that was insured by God, He was completely covered. Do you realize every time you* win a battle, it's another testimony. Every time you overcome one thing it is your strength to endure another. And every time David exercised His gifts for the Lord, God increased his coverage. David continued to try to please God and God continued to look after David. As God Anoint you, then you will be immediately set completely apart from the rest and you will become a peculiar person. You will have gone through something in your life that you know only God had brought you through. Can't nobody testify about it like you can. Surely, in your life there will be some very life noticeable changes. Exodus 19:5 says, Now therefore, if ye will obey my voice indeed, and keep my covenant, then ye shall be a peculiar treasure unto me above all people; for all the earth is mine.

Somethings you use to do, they will no longer be of interest to you. Some people you use to hang with, you won't be able to withstand there company any more. If God were for you, then who cares who is against you. Your life intention will be *finally focused on pleasing God, because now you will know the full consequences of not pleasing Him. Your day's journey will begin in praise from the heart for God, all because you can't forget just how far He has brought you from.* ***Awe can't you feel that Anointing brewing in your gifts. Can you feel that unspeakable joy flowing all through your heart?*** *God is a God worth praising? I have heard this over and over, I want to shout but I can't. Baby, when I just look back over my life – I shout. It doesn't take me to look back too far, the Lord has blessed me so much. I have been through the wringer, if only you knew. My breathe is worth a praise. To have my family living under the same roof is a praise. For me to utilize my right side from being paralized is a praise. I have more than enough reasons to praise Him. I can imagine why David loved to praise, His wartimes was great and his battles were even greater, but the Lord allowed him not only to survive but to be a winner. David had to constantly prove, the he served a Mighty and Awesome God. Every battle, every war and every* *victory. Psalm 55:16 says, As for me, I will call upon God; and the Lord shall save me.*

It is so wonderful that He has thought enough of you, I consider it a life set up. Remember all the times you felt so down that you couldn't get up, wasn't it God that set you up. All those times that you thought you were not going to ever be worth anything, look at how God thought more of you than you have ever thought of yourself. That downfall that you went through was just for God to Anoint the Works of Your Hands. Perhaps if things in your life would have never happened like they have, then God would have never been able to give you this vision. Thank Him for every down fall because only He has set you up. God wants you to receive His promises and obey what He tells you because He has some treasures waiting on you that money just can't buy. Psalm 25:14 says, The secret of the Lord is with them that fear him; and he will show them his covenant. David was covered because He knew how to inspire God. He satisfied

God with his praise as he continuously gave God his undivided attention. During Davids praise, it was God's time, as he song it was God's time and as he worshipped it was God's time. David didn't let anything or anyone interuupt his time to share with God. His praise was his proof, that The Almighty was his life protector. He caressed God's heart in the manner he praised and utilized his gifts. He proved to God just how much he truly appreciated Him.

This Power is not a Power of man, or of self-flesh but it is a Power of Affliction, that is forever lasting. You cannot run from the Anointing Powers of God no matter how hard you try. It will cause your heart to agree with the Spirit of God. You will do things that you never thought, that you would be able to do. You will then, be able to touch people and they will be instantly healed. As you speak, The Spirit of God will be your life speaker. As you open your mouth, even the death shall hear. What so ever you begin to speak, it all shall come to pass. Your hands will do works that it never dreamed of. Your eyes will see larger and your dreams will expand until it will cause you to make a move. Your visions will grow within your Spirit that will cause a multitude to be saved. 1John 2:27 says, But the anointing which ye have received of him abideth in you, and ye need not that any man teach you: but as the same anointing teacheth you all things, and is truth, and is no lie, and even as it taught you, ye shall abide in him.

You will not even have to open your mouth for the WORDS of God to speak. As you walk you will be a lighthouse for the lost, you will be a doctor in the sick room, alone just by being present. The enemy will fear you as you walk, he will flee out of your way as he feel your presence drawing nearer and to sum it all up - you will simply scare hell to death. You will destroy the tricks of the enemy. You will steal the life out of hell as you place your feet on the ground in the presence of your enemies. Psalm 23:5 says, Thou preparest a table before me in the presence of mine enemies: thou anointest my head with oil; my cup runneth over. You will kill the lies out of every deceitful life that you are around. **The Anointing is contagious;** *it will cause others that are connected in your presence to feel the sensation of it. It is like an air born disease, it will touch anyone that gets in its way just to let them know that it is contagious and All - Powerful. Truly many people do not understand the Anointing, they think because they shout from time to time that they have felt the Anointing. On the other hand, if they get a little too emotional some time they have experienced the Anointing. If they cry in service and cannot stop, they thought they felt the Anointing. Well I am here to tell you that is not the Anointing. The Anointing comes once The Hands of the Lord is Upon You. The Anointing is the yoke destroyer and there will be a true change that will take place in your life. I am speaking of behind the close door changes, that you know only the Lord knows about. This change will begin secretly just between you and the Lord.*

*Just because you have felt feverless hot at times, that wasn't the anointing. Though fire had ran through your inner soul, or you fell out in the midst of a worship service, well that isn't the Anointing either. Once the Anointing comes upon you, it will put a Spirit of righteousness deep inside you. **The Anointing will grow at large until it consumes the flesh up out of you**. The Anointing will destroy the yokes inside of you, fry it up, flip it over and eat it up until all the yokes are gone. It is time for you to claim your acceptable year of the Lord. **God is getting ready to give it all to you, through the life of your work, life more abundantly, life over flowing and life posing all power. Are you truly ready for this New Life Production?** Psalm 34:1 says, I Will bless the Lord at all times: his praise shall continually be in your mouth. David had numerous reasons to praise, and he knew his praise was only for God. No one ever had to persuade him to go and serve God, he knew who he served. David's heart was always in preparation to praise God. He didn't allow his troubles, problems, battles* *or even sin stop his praise. You will be amazed how powerful God praise can be, it will cause the flood gates of heaven to pour out abundance for you. It will consume your enemies and cause your battles to be won. It will give you heavenly power, meaning the doors in your life will begin to open that no man will ever have the power to shut. That is why David was so blessed, because he constantly praised His God. He knew that he simply owed God His praise. The greater your praise, the greater your victory. David praise report was so long, sometimes he couldn't tell it all, so therefore he had to dance out the rest. When you realize the hell that God has removed out of your life, no one will ever have to persuade you to praise Him. It will utter itself out of you. When you realize how powerful your God is, then a worry will not be on your mind, but your victory praise will. David was a sure praiser, he knew his God deserved praise every time he just thought of his goodness. Haven't God been a wonderful God to you, awesome I know. Just remember to give Him His praise, those are His* praises and not yours. He is worthy and at all times His praise I do owe Him. Just as you desire your blessings, He desire His praise – it's His glory. So excuse me, if you see me in a grocery store, giving Him His praise. Just ignore me if you see me at a stop light giving Him His praise. I most definetly owe Him my life, because the hell alone that He has brought me through. I'm going to give Him His praise. Those are His praises, not mine. No one can do me like He has – what about you? I once ran into this Apostle that thought I was a babe in Christ, surely I am. One thing about a child, is that they are always prepared to listen to their guardians. A child will be obedient and they knew the consequences of dis-obedience. David was one that continued in his child like faith. He never grew too large for God, or too high that he couldn't praise Him. I also felt like David. No one knows the troubles I have been through, and no one could praise Him like I can. The many storms that He has carried me through, believe me I owe Him my praise. When everyone turned their back on me, He was there. He has truly *being my high tower I owe Him praise. Often times many will begin to gain so much, until now they will feel as though they are too grown too praise. Well David always allowed his heart to stay as a child's heart towards God, that is why his praise greatly satisfied heaven. A child is always excited to see their daddy and David was always excited to glorify his Heavenly Father. Allow praise to continually be in your mouth, uplift and inspire God, after all He rightfully deserve to always be praised.*

Chapter Six

Maintain Your Coverage

You must know who you are to the Lord, David knew who he was. He was a chief musician, one that was skillful and great. He was also a warrior with many recorded defeats. He was a praiser, that loved to dance. On the other hand, he also had a lot of spiritual distractions that tried to hinder his progress. His heart poured out as he arranged the worship services of the temple. Yes, he was a worship instructor too. And I wondered for many of years, why was he so blessed despite all of his sins. One thing I realized about God, He doesn't put his focus on our sins, but He notices our inner being. God knows exactly who we are through our hearts intentions. 1 Chronicles 6:31 says, And these are they whom David set over the service of song in the house of the LORD, after the ark had rest. No matter who you are, we all need to maintain our coverage in the LORD. Sin is so easy to entangle in, most of the time you will commit it and then realize it later. It is strong and it's purpose is to stop us from worshipping our Lord. David wasn't no fool he knew that too. Sin has a power that only you yourself can give, don't feed it your soul. No one can overcome sin, Without The Lord – No One! Sin only wants to feed your mind the many reasons not to serve the Lord, so that perhaps it can stop your worship. Worship is all powerful, it will release every strong enemy and cause them to flee out of your life. Now think of once your enemies are out of your way, nothing will stop you from excelling in life. And once you excel in life, your praise will excel too. However, your worship will excel and God's Glory will be exalted - more through you. That is the full purpose of sin is to control your praise – the enemy wants to STEAL, KILL & DESTROY your Worship and Praise from the LORD. Hasn't he taken enough from you, look at your life – He isn't worth one more thing not even your praise and worship. Give God His Praise and ADORATION and watch how He will remove all of your enemies. Understand in our life time we all must endure somethings, that are going to break us down or either identify who we are. Every battle I had to fight was a battle that trained me for more, encouraged me for greater and a test that I had past. When life punches come at you, the majority of times they are unexpected. Yes, it hurts, but you must fight back. David was able to stand against so much, because he knew how to inspire God. He was a true worshipper and his worship kept him covered. No matter what rose up against David or perhaps what kind of sin he had encountered, he adored utilizing his gifts to satisfy God. No one had to convince David that he was one of the greatest warriors, greatest faith walkers and greatest psalmist. David knew that he was nothing without his LORD, he knew his Savior.

Don't let no one tell you any different. I once knew this person and he tried to persuade me of somethings about while we shouldn't go to church. I too had been hurt in the church, but he didn't understand all that the LORD has brought me through. This conversation we had wasn't explanatory to me, because I knew JESUS. As I told him during my troubles, I called on the name of JESUS and He heard my cry. When my children was deeply in the need, I called on the name of JESUS and He was my way maker. When people spitefully criticized and used me I called on the name of JESUS, He was there. No other has blessed me as He has. No matter what I have done in my life, no other has forgiven me as He has and no one can love me as He can. All my life I called on His name and He has continuously saved me.

Regardless of what man is trying or thinking that they are doing to the house of God, I'm going to give God His praise. I will not withhold my Heavenly Father from His praise. It's like stealing and I didn't want to be a thief. There is nothing like the power of The Most High and He is sweet I know.

David was the one that arranged worship for the house of the LORD. He was the minister of music, able to excite the hearts of the congregation. He caused hearts to praise as they worshipped. He was the one that introduced the congregation to worship as he ministered in song. He was a true praiser and his praises he gave to his LORD. Can you imagine, being the one that will cause people to notice God less known worship HIM. Well David, soothe the hearts of many as he caused them to worship His Heavenly Father. 1 Chronicles 6:32 says, And these are they whom David set over the service of song in the house of the LORD, after that the ark had rest. He had a

purpose to introduce them to His Heavenly Father,
David knew of spiritual distractions. He knew how
hard it was just to enter into the gates of His
Heavenly Father. David heavily encountered many
problems. He was being spiritually tormented in
many ways. The enemy wanted to stopDavid from
ever receiving all that God had promised him. The
enemy tried everything he could to get David to not
go forth. That is why his battles was so great, the
enemy was hoping that during one of his wartimes
that someone would kill him. If you notice David,
even as a child being the One that destroyed a
powerful Giant, it caused others to question their
faith. As many looked upon David, they saw true
victories of his God. Truly He caused many to
marvel as they probably said, " How did he do
that". Well God wants the same effect from your
life, He wants to take the giants in your life out –
but you must maintain your coverage. Notice, David
was being empowered every time he was able to
minister in music. David was being feed every time
he was being preached to. David also was being

encouraged, just alone by entering the gates. In addition, he was completely rejuvenated to be prepared for whats to come, he gained new strength. There is so much when you enter into The Presence of The LORD. I don't know about you, but there is nothing like taking a moment out of your busy day just to adore your God. See, David knew Him as his all and all. He rescued David more times than any other recorded in the bible. He blessed David through the greatest battles to win and have the victory. Despite all of David's spiritual distractions, he still took the time to praise and worship God. I can only testify to what I know, living life trying to overcome is extremely challenging and I can't do it by myself – what about you? As we go through life strong holds, we must maintain our coverage. It is a time that we must truly prove our faith, we must stand. When that day comes in your life and you are pushed into a brick wall, you can't step backwards. You must be determined to move forward, despite that wall and any other spiritual distractions. You can only depend on supernatural strength with an expectancy to be moved. David did and he was moved each time. You will just simply need a Miracle Worker, David did and he received many. Often times we get into those kind of situations, but in the midst we need to maintain our coverage. David assembled all the time in the house of The LORD, utilizing his gift for God kept him covered. I'm not perfect, neither are you. We all fall short of His Glory sometimes - we all need to be inspired, uplifted, motivated and encouraged to run on. The house of the LORD is where you can stay covered. I once heard this Apostle say, keep your problems out of the house of the LORD! I wondered who was this Apostle serving, from that day forward. Understand that the house of the LORD is a "Spiritual Hospital", it's a place for spiritual healing, spiritual deliverance and spiritual motivation. So that is why I believe David stayed covered, he knew the house of the LORD was his spiritual hospital. He was spiritually sick and he needed spiritually deliverance. He was spiritually wounded and he needed to be spiritually healed. He was spiritually broken and he needed to be spiritually mended. Gathering with the saints may not look like that much to you, but it was everything to David and he stayed covered. When you enter into sin, it is a spiritual distraction and there is only way to remove it – it is with The Spirit of God. Overcoming life obstacles and sin is a spiritual warfare. David had to allow the Pressence of The Lord to cleanse him from sin, that is why praise continuosly came out of his mouth. He knew that he wasn't perfect, he was a sinner and he didn't try to hide it. Psalms 37:4 says, Delight thyself also in the LORD; and he shall give thee the desires of thine heart.

If David could hold on to nothing else, he held on to this word. If I delight myself in God, He will give me the desires of my heart. David continuously tried to prove to God that he was delighting himself in Him. Everything David needed, only God had the power to produce. Man couldn't possibly posses Davids future, he desired *things that money couldn't purchase. David desired a title that required more than what he currently had. He needed conquering power, great integrity, substantial stability and all that would fit with a title of becoming a KING. His heart desire was greater than what he had, so therefore God had to allow his challenges to bring forth many great victories. All of David's test was to prepare him for the life, the power and wealthy lifestyle of becoming a King. So therefore, your heart desires will sometimes cause your life challenges to be more than you can bear just to spiritually equip you with what you truly will need to succeed.*

David desired some great things of the LORD, just think of all he had to endure. Just as you must endure, you too must desire to come out. Sometimes, your coming out is harder than your going through period and the strength alone that you will need is powerful. Well David was a great warrior and he needed power to overcome, strength to battle and will power to suceed. Just imagine war after war, battle after battle and victory each time. Yes, David was extremely wealthy in faith as he continuously proved to God that He was his LORD. How many times have you quit proving to God, utilizing your gifts or making excuses all because of someone or something. It is not worth it, because God can't receive no glory out of that. There have been many times I too was angry and didn't want to go to church because of something or someone. Or prepahs, there was things I needed to do, but I didn't because of something or someone. Truly, I was only hindering my own progress. I no longer wanted my blessings to be aborted. Often times we are so close to our next breakthrough, we are literally able to touch it - but we quit and give up too soon. Our excuses are not worth it, we only abort our own prosperity.

Do you remember hearing from the LORD at all? Well a lot of times he has spoken to me in a form of prosperity and His word was so fulfilling. It has caused me to expect these things to *come to pass, what about you? I decided not to give up that easily just because my life looked like it was in a rumble. No, I decided to fight for what I believed in. The Lord has spoken too many wonderful things into my hearing, if you only knew the half of what I had to endure. Life can be extremely challenging at times, it can make you question yourself as well as prove your faith. Though hell has occasionally rose up in my life, I had to allow my faith to exceed to the next level - anyhow. Listen, God is speaking to you.*

David was one that heard his voice, even through his spiritual distractions. 11 Samuel 22:20 says, He brought me forth also into a large place: he delivered me, because he delighted in me. David knew Him as a DELIVERER, know Him as your DELIVERER. He will bring you out into a place to call your own. No one will be able to claim your land, your territory and not even your blessings. As God blessed David, everyone was able to see and say that The Lord's Hands was upon him.

Continue to use what the LORD has given you and excel in life. Stop allowing people, things, circumstances and situations to cause spiritual distractions to stop you. If you have too many spiritual distractions where you are, then relocate because your future is depending on it. Every distraction in your life is a hindrance and sometimes you must go. David knew the LORD had delivered him from his strong enemy, he wasn't expecting to be held back any longer. Just as he eventually became King, you too will eventually succeed just as long as you maintain your coverage. Allow God to receive His glory and watch how He will keep you covered. Regardless of your circumstances, situations, battles and spiritual distractions, He got you covered. The battle is not yours it is the Lord's, so what are you worried about? 11 Samuel 22:30 says, For by thee I have run through a troop: by my God have I leaped over a wall. Allow God to cause you to leap over walls, to run with victory and see what your end is going to be. All that he did forDavid, He can do it for you *too, just maintain your coverage for your future*

depends on it.

Chapter Seven

Your Destiny Is Packed In Your Gift

What intentions do you have for your life, that is the key to unwrapping your gift? I know some people do not have big goals set for their lives, perhaps some can't see no farther than where they are. If you notice, most of them aren't word believers either, because most of us realize that with faith all things are truly possible. Truly I have claimed some beautiful and expensive things in my lifetime, actually more than my normal income could possibly purchase. Only my faith could deliver me, so therefore I realized I had to utilize my gifts. Your destiny is packed in your gift *and your heart will lead you to your destiny, if you follow it.*

*Psalm 84:11 says, For the Lord God is a sun and shield: the Lord will give grace and glory: no good thing will he withhold from them that walk uprightly. **Keep your promises in your sight, never letting them go**. The Lord rewards those that deserves it. As long as you know that you are doing something that deserves to be awarded, then expect one. Occasionally go by and put claims on things that you can't afford, but that your heart desires. Touch somethings that are tasteful and good, want them with a passion. Post them up in your eyesight. Just stay reminded of everything that God said, He was going to do for you. God spoke to me when I was going through and I could not see my way out. My eyes saw darkness, but my heart felt the light. My bank account was negative, but God told me I was rich. My bills were over due, but God told me they were paid. I claimed things that my money could not buy* in a 10-year life span, but God said you are going to be able to pay cash for it. **He is a God of His word and His word is true**. There are some things you must keep in your eyesight. It is just like a child wanting candy, and as long as they can crave the sweetness, they will do what you tell them to do. Post it up on your mirror, in your kitchen, office or perhaps on your car dash board- just keep it in your sight. As long as you can keep your eyes on the prize, then you will run and not get tired. You will recognize the power that is in your gift(s). Your faith will grow because you will be able to keep your hope alive. Keep your visions in your sight, hold on to them. Post it where you can see it everyday. **Allow your goals to be seen by your eyes and think of your end result**. Stand on it and don't be moved, no matter how hard times get; just hold on to your prize as if you have already have won it. When you hold on to it in that manner, then you will finish what you have started. If you hold on to it as if you already have it, then you are walking through the finish line with your arms up. **God Is Waiting**

On You At The Finish Line. *Ecclesiastes 9:11 says, I returned, and saw under the sun, that the race is not to the swift, nor the battle to the strong, neither yet bread to the wise, nor yet riches to men of understanding, nor yet favor to men of skill; but time and chance happened to them all. God wants you to know that He is waiting on you at the finish line and He wants His praise once you complete this task. This is your chance to get it right, so that He can bless you righteously. He wants to give you – your heart desires. He has your new life waiting at the finish line, He is routing for you to run on. Your hope for tomorrow is in every forward step that you make to the finish line today. The harder you run the more hope you'll gain. Your joy unspeakable is right here at the finish line. If you could ask Isaiah, Job and Abraham how did they make it – surely they will tell you it wasn't easy. God is sure that they will tell you to keep moving forward, hold on to your faith and through it all just trust God. They kept stepping forth and they did not let anything stop them. Though times they may have* *tarried, and times they may have come to a halt but they never stopped taking their steps forward. Though sin sometimes may have gotten them off the right track, it was the love of God that routed them to there finish line. Though the road was hard and sometimes they got discouraging, they never threw in their towel of hope, they kept on moving anyhow. They kept their eyes prepared and ready to see the finish line of faith. Your prosperity is at the finish line, your wealth and all your promises are waiting on you at the finish line. All those things that you have ever imagined good to happen in your life, right at the end of your finish line - along with every heart drenching prayer that you have poured out your heart. It is all waiting and prepared just for you. By the way, He said the more laps you run the sooner you will get to the finish line. The more effort you put in the works of your hands, the sooner you will be finished with it. Regardless of your skills, God can use them for His glory. He wants you to take what you have and run with it, regardless of the length just run on.* **No matter how** *fit you are for this journey; continue to allow Gods Anointing Power to get you in perfect shape*. That vision, that dream, that gift is all yours because God gave it to you. Now, move with it, step in it and live it to the fullness because Gods Anointing Power is in it. He wants your hands on it, so that you can truly live your acceptable year of the Lord.

Isaiah 61:2 says, To proclaim the acceptable year of the Lord, and vengeance of our God; to comfort all that mourn. Now God is transforming all of your nothings into something. He is bringing forth the evidence that He has heard your cry. All those long nights that you yielded your heart unto Him, you poured out from your belly the hell that has tormented you. In addition, all those enemies that stole your possessions, took the things you love for a selfish gain. They tried to destroy you, God said it is pay back time. Romans 12:14 says, Bless them which persecute you: bless and not curse. As He visits your enemies, He will let them know why he is serving an eviction notice on all of *their belongings. He will let them know that they stole some valuable things from you. He will cause them to have to come unto you with blessings and good deeds seeking your forgiveness. God will restore everything that was taken out of your life for a purpose and as He restores these things unto you, they will come to you bigger and better than before. It is your Hallelujah shouting time, because the victory is now yours. You have worked with expectancy that this was your acceptable year of the Lord, and your faith says it is so. Once you realize without a shadow of a doubt that God expects the works of your hands to posses His anointing powers, then you will work it like never before. All those that mourned when you mourned, prayed and cried along by your side will receive the overflow of your blessings, they too will be restored. Oh, now He is straightening out some crooked stuff within your enemies that caused you to cry and that upset you. It is just as a child that got beat up by that neighborhood bully and ran home to tell their daddy, boy a daddy don't let no one beat up their child and get away with it. That daddy is going to be like a wolf. He's going to straighten out the bully, and as they see the daddy coming down the street they are going to know that trouble is on it's way. Immediately, they will begin to fear. So don't worry about your enemies. Because God will have the vengeance of them, your battles and all of your enemies. In addition, as God exercise the vengeance on them He will bring you back all their possessions that they have sitting at their gates. Um what a beautiful effect, because you don't have to say a word or even get angry. God will have all vengeance against every enemy that has ever come up against you. Because when they went against you they messed around with a child of God. That is why Satan is sitting in hell right now, because He messed around with God. The enemy forgot that Jesus has the keys to hell and guess what, He is your vindicator. Just as long as you are in God and He is in you, then you too posses those same keys to hell. I mean every part of it, so do not worry. Romans 12:19 says, Dearly beloved, avenge not yourselves, but rather give place unto wrath: for it is written, Vengeance is mine; I will repay, saith the Lord.*

Just keep in mind that God did it all for you. He remembered every heavy load, every burden that you carried and every weight that you lifted while you was trying all that you had. Just because many hurt you as you tried, God does not ever want you to turn out to be another one of them. He wants you to always walk in love, kindness and to do many good deeds as a righteous warrior that has won the battle. God is going to turn your whole entire life around. The work of your hands is going to prove to many that the Hands of The Lord Is Upon You. It will be noticeable to all to see that God is in you. So therefore continue to represent God as a God of Love. Represent in a right manner, be a true God ambassador and be on your best conduct at all times, with anyone and any situation. Romans 12:21 says, Be not overcome of evil, but overcome evil with good.

A Precious Gift From God

For every time that you were confused and you were brought to shame, God is going to grant you a double to a hundred – fold return. Your reward will be your inheritance, it is calculated through your portion of faith. If you grow large in faith, then your portion will be great. If you only have minute faith, then your inheritance portion will be little. However, if your faith has no limits on how much God can bless you, then your inheritance will never quit calculating. Literally meaning by the time you will leave the face of this earth, that absolutely no one will be able to sum up your increase. Remember, what He had told you, well now it is at an all time high; just as if the stock market has hit the top of the roof and your increase breaks through. God is going to grant you more than you can imagine for all your troubles. Your acceptable year is the year that God will find and bestow the favor of increase upon you. Every stronghold that has bounded you down through every locked down and imprisoned situation, God said, "Its your FREEDOM TIME". Heaven is about to release every promise that God promised you, just because you held out and held on. God is unlocking every locked up blessing that kept you from prospering. You know all those dreams that you have had and God brought forth a new covenant, well it is pay day time, pay back time and over pay time. Your gain is going to be larger than your eyes could ever see, why because you trusted in the Lord to be your help in the midnight hour. When everyone belittled you, laughed at you and scandalized you – you held on. Why? Because you have been crazy enough to believe in all these wild crazy faith feeling dreams that God was going to do this thing for you and through you. So therefore, God is going to give you every desire of your heart; including the desires that you have forgotten about. Isaiah 61:8 says, For I the LORD love judgment, I hate robbery for burnt offering; and I will direct their work in truth, and I will make an everlasting covenant with them.

Now you know that God has Anointed your hands for this work because it is now being fruitful and multiplying, if it have not yet then it will. Only God can cause such an enrichment of prosperity and joy to come into your life. God loves satisfying with the truth, that is why the truth shall set you free. As one of my good friends mother always say, Baby one thing God loves, it ain't nothing but the truth, I tell you that's what He loves". His Anointing Powers has the key that is going to cause those closed doors to open as you begin to walk towards them. When the tree of David had been cut down, the stump still had life in it. Though many things seemed to try to cut down the works of your hands, it still has a life form of power because God owns the root of it. In addition, as long as God is connected to the root, then what are you worried about; your vision is going to live. It is going to grow, you do not have to water it, because God is going to water it with His increase. Just as the seeds have already been sown, your ground has already begun its tilling process and a seed cannot

A Precious Gift From God

sit but so long. After your seed take ground root, no matter what seed you sewed, it shall spring forth and as the buds sprout their way out of the ground it will burst up and burst threw. Now you wont be able to see that day as it burst through the ground, you may look one day and still see no bud coming forth, but if you look again you'll see the bud sitting right there. It literally snuck it's way through while you wasn't looking. Every thing that you have sowed through your effort, through your will power, through your determination and through your diligent work - God will direct an order per seed you have sown. All seeds must burst through, all seeds have a time to grow and your seeds are getting ready to grow. God wants you to have all new fruit in your life. The Anointing Powers that are in Your Hands are going to produce new fruit in your life, are you ready?

Most people look at judgment as a bad thing, but from God fearing believers we shall receive a righteous reward. God will judge you for *everything that you did right.* **He will set an everlasting promise with you that will be made accordingly as He decide what you deserves.**

I believe God for the covenant that He has made in my life, no man can tare me from it because I want my promises and the land it sets on to flow with milk and honey. **God's promises are true.** *God loves to be satisfied with good works and as you satisfy God with the Works of Your Hands He will allow you more favor. He will fulfill His promises to you. The more you satisfy Him is the more power, He will give you to do greater works.* **God is a God of increase, a God of faithfulness and a God that will establish wonderful works.** *As you prove to God that you are faithful in your work, He will fulfill your vision to be at large, He will grant you every true reward because He has accepted your work with gladness in His heart. It is a wonderful thing when we satisfy God, because He fulfills our every need and He will not rest until He properly satisfies you.*

*Isaiah 61:11 says, For as the earth bringeth forth her bud, and as the garden causeth the things that are sown in it to spring forth; so the Lord GOD will cause **righteousness and praise to spring forth before all the nations.***

*I pray that this book has brought you in to your favorable year of the Lord **"ACCEPTABLE YEAR OF THE LORD"** and that it has been more than you ever expected it to be in your life. This is your year for you to expect things you've only dreamed of to appear in yor life. It is valuable that you work with the Anointing Powers that God has given you. Utilize your gifts and keep them covered. There are many accomplishments to be made by the works of your hands and the vision(s) that God has assigned unto you. **I believe in The Anointing Powers of God and that no hands can accomplish a greater work without The Anointing**. Keep in mind that every seed that you have sown, through your work dedication, effort, self will, monetary, and so on that God is going to release your ground* *with the buds of all of your sown seeds. Some seeds you may have forgotten that you sowed and not all you can count, just let God do the calculations while you send up your praises. Very soon it is all going to make men as well as you- say Awe. We serve an AWESOME GOD. The hands of the Lord are upon you and the Anointing Powers Are in your Hands. Use them for His Glory and He shall bless your gift(s) as He shall receive greater glory. Praise Him for He is Worthy and praise Him for all your buds springing forth fruit in your land of increase. Rejoice, because this is Your Acceptable Year of The Lord. Though many things in your life seemed to be empty, God is going to fulfill them all. This is your year where you shall gain favorable increase, so rejoice and be glad.*

One night as I was talking to my aunt Pauline, we were discussing happiness. At that time, I had so many wrong things going on in my life, until I forgot all about being happy. I was trying so hard to make everyone else happy until I simply forgot about myself. Through our conversation she said, "baby have you ever prayed for happiness." I thought for a minute and I realized I wanted to be happy, but I never desired to be happy. It hit me from that day forward. As I thought more and more about happiness, I realized I thought of some things that would make me happy. My happiness was not in things, because things can't love you back. You know sometimes we can think if God bless us with something that we have wanted that it will make us happy. Well that is not true. Because as soon as you get it, the newness will fade away and then you will find yourself starting over and over again wanting something else. I thought of many things that would really make me happy, but it was The One that God had given me, that truly caused my happiness. This gift contains joy late in the midnight hour, more valuable than gold, the brightest light that will never dim, dominion with all power, nothing will ever top this gift. It is too valuable to price and not everyone can

A Precious Gift From God

receive it, though it is one of a kind. It is the largest, most beautiful and powerful gift you will ever receive and He wants your appreciation. In this gift, it is power to conquer, your beginning and end. Jesus is the light in your darkest hours and life for eternity. Though His gift took many years to develop as it still is developing today through our faith, as we grow stronger in the Lord. Know that Jesus paid the ultimate price. Yes God gave Him the Gift of becoming our Savior, but Jesus still had to put His hands on the Gift. He unwrap it, appreciated it and He took the time to share it with us. Try to understand where it all come from. On the cross when He commended Himself to God, He Gave JEHOVAH all that He Had and for that alone JEHOVAH gave Him All Power. Jesus always showed great Honor towards His Heavenly Father. Just as Jesus rose up you can too with your Precious Gift from God, through the Blood of Jesus the Christ. He is your Opportunity to the tree of Life. Utilize your gift, and use this opportunity to gain the greatest life you can. This is your opportunity take advantage of it, utilize this chance. Be blessed, be a praiser and become a victorious warrior. Remember whatever you desire, whatever you seek after is what will find. So therefore seek after the right things and watch how He will ultimately bless your life. Also note, your destiny is packed in your gift, so unwrap it and show it to the world.

The End

A Precious Gift From God

Parice C. Parker

A Prayer For You To Gain The Anointing

Our Heavenly Father that is full with righteousness, full with mercy and grace - please Anoint the Works of my hands. Forgive my heart of all my wrong doings, Oh Heavenly Father make me right. Give me The Right Spirit that will make me right, allow the love of Jesus to cleanse my heart and make me pure. Keep me daily away from all temptations and strengthen me greater as I kneel in prayer. Allow my voice to sing acceptable praises unto you, that will make me fall deeper in love with you. Teach me your secrets Lord, withhold no good thing from me. Though Lord I can't depend on my self, surely I will trust you with all of me. Jesus teach me how to trust you. A work that I must do, make it right within me. Anoint me Lord, Anoint my head with your precious Holy Oil. Allow all the angels in heaven to pray over me, and touch my enemies and make them flee. Anoint me Lord give me the power over all of my enemies. Give me strength in every weakness, Lord Anoint Me with

A Precious Gift From God

your glory. Teach me Lord, be my guide, lead me Lord guide my feet, lay your hands upon me. In the name of Jesus, I pray this Prayer, give me an answer Lord that you have answered this prayer and as you Anoint me Bless Me to be that everlasting blessing for your Glory, so that many will see that you are JEHOVAH - JIREH and they will desire to please your heart. Allow this gift that you have given me to be your inspiration, teach me Lord how to inspire you; so that I can inspire millions and lead them all to you.

AMEN, AMEN & AMEN

Proverbs 10:22 says, The Blessings of the Lord, it maketh rich, and he addeth no sorrow with it.

<u>*My Personal Testimony*</u>

One day the Lord spoke to me, He told me so many wonderful things I just laughed. For many of years the enemy has tried to keep me from receiving all those wonderful things that The Lord told me. He has attacked me at every angle in my life, but God spared me to be a living witness. I write because He fills my heart, I sing because He makes me happy and I am a believer because He has been my Life Instructor. When you really want to become more than a conquer, you will not let doubt, embarrassment, being a failure, a bruise, hurt, shame, sin or anything stop you from receiving your reward. He has a way of bringing forth our blessings and they are in our gifts. Let your gift excel unto you reach your destiny.

Books Written By Parice Parker

Living Life In A Messed Up Situation – Volume One

Living Life In A Messed Up Situation – Volume Two

The Anointing Powers Of Your Hands

A Precious Gift From God

Aggravated Assault On Your Mind

Coming Soon

I'm A Certified Stroke Survivor

It Ain't What It Looks Like

Order Your Books On Line or

Check Your Nearest Bookstore

www.booksfolph.com

All Orders Will Be Immediately Shipped Out

Thanks For Your Business

The Exit Thought:

Often times we do not even realize the value of our gifts. God gives us gifts of a remembrance, for something supernaturally special. Regardless the occasion or even if we don't always deserve them, He still finds a particular reason to give us gifts. The majority of the times we don't even appreciate them. Every gift that is given unto us is to Glorify God. His gifts represent just how powerful He is, who He is and that He is. Have you ever received a gift and didn't even say thank you or failed to realize how special that gift was that was given unto you? Soon afterwards, the person that gave you that particular gift - feelings were hurt, because they noticed that you didn't even take the time to appreciate it. There's a reason and something special behind every gift that you have received in your lifetime or given. To others it may not have cost a lot of money, but truly it was special to them. Think for a moment when you have been low on funds and you go out your way to present a *gift to someone and they don't even take the time to appreciate it. However, to you it was all you had and you went out your way. Surely you could have kept your money and not even showed up for the occasion, but you did. I believe we make God feel that exact same way many of times, by not appreciating our gifts. God has gifted you with something unique that money just can't buy. His Son paid an ultimate cost with His Precious Blood, just for God to please you. What more can you ask for? Prove to God how much you appreciate your gift and inspire Him!*

Proverbs 10:22

Proverbs 10:22 says, The Blessings of the Lord, it maketh rich, and he addeth no sorrow with it.
As soon as you appreciate the gift(s) that God has given you, then you will begin to adore all of your prosperity possibilities. Eventually He will give you a vision to incorporate your gift, you make Him proud and He will make you happy. Use what He has given you and you will receive His blessings. In

addition, once you receive His blessings; then everything you will begin to put your hands on will be blessed. Your gifts will greatly prosper you, especially knowingly the amount of glory He is going to receive from you. Remember He deserves His Glory, so therefore Give It To Him.

Be Richly Blessed, In Jesus Name.

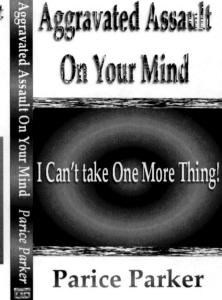

Aggravated Assault On Your Mind

All your life, you only wanted their love, attention, and affection of appreciation shown towards you in a heart-felt way of tender moments. Instead, you receive everything you do not deserve such as attitudes un adjusted, occasions of feeling aggravated, and definitely irritable due towards their insincerity of devotion to you. Regardless of your situation never let it destroy you, shake the dust off and move forward.

Once again my heart has been clawed. Truly I realized after the agony I had to experience I was born to write. Truly my hell was purposed for another to be inspired. Life is almost like a football game, there will be one winner and one loser always, but I choose to win. Welcome to a snap shot of Aggravated Assault On Your Mind, you are not alone.

BN 09787162-3-X

Title:
Aggravated Assault On Your Mind
Author: Parice Parker

Pages: 420
Price: $19.95

When you are so aggravated about real life issues, and everything falls on you. Your friends, love ones and family just do not appreciate all that you have tried to do. You need what you need and you have giving all you can,... simply thinking, then what is the use?
 Let Those Aggravations Cause You To Be Blessed Indeed, Get this one !!!

ISBN 09787162-1-3

Title:
The Anointing Powers Of Your Ha
Author: **Parice Parker**

Pages: **206**
Price: **$13.95**

The Anointing Powers of Your Han
will cause you to reach for things i
life, that will amaze every eye tha
looks at you - including yourself. I
you have a vision and it seems a
though it's not coming forth, this bo
is for you. Get your copy today an
Triumph with Victory tomorrow.
This is your vision enhancer, this
one is for you!!!!!!

Motivational Speaking Engagements &
correspondence please mail to:
Parice Parker Ministries
P. O. Box 680475
Charlotte, N. C. 28216
Email: www.pariceparker@yahoo.com
No Charge, for the price has already been paid.
Attention: Parice Parker Ministries